Mindful Meditations in Nature

By
Jodi Winter & Rebecca Winter

Contents

Introduction

Welcome to our little book of mindful meditations in nature. This book has been compiled to include some of our most popular and enjoyable meditations.

We have drawn upon our own experiences of a variety of meditation styles and traditions to form our own library of go to meditations for all situations and timescales.

Under normal circumstances, you will find us in a small clearing in the woodlands of Moira Furnace Museum & Country Park in North West Leicestershire at the heart of The National Forest. We will be surrounded by a group of fellow nature lovers and meditators. Our weekly mediation sessions have grown in popularity over the last three years, and we now have a fantastic group that are there every week and have formed a collective mind, often experiencing shared emotions, messages and characters.

Wild Minds was just an idea at the tail end of 2019. We had plans to launch a new business in 2020, but the world had other plans and we had to hold off for a short while. Our initial aim was to create fun and interactive sessions for families to attend, to re-connect them with each other and with nature. To remove technology (if only for a short while) and to get the next generation outdoors, learning and exploring through their senses. However, when we were able to get things fully up and running following lockdown, we opened up the woodland to meditation. There has been a weekly interaction of people and nature ever since.

We have spent the last couple of years creating, practicing and delivering our own meditations to a wide range of people of all ages and with varying degrees of meditation experience. We have come to appreciate the natural world around us much more and have started to see collective experiences in groups of meditators who practice together regularly. This really is a phenomenal result, and we can only thank nature for her part in it.

The practice of meditation is as old as the human race itself. Meditation can come in many forms and can be practiced by everyone at any time. To meditate is to find inner peace, even if just in that moment. To continue to practice meditation is to fill your life with happiness. To enable you to find happiness in the little things and to let external noise and distraction pass you by. Meditation allows you to develop a moment of stillness in even the strongest of storms, to remain as constant and as strong as an anchor in a wild sea.

In the coming chapters, we will introduce you to a selection of the meditations you would get to experience if you were in the woods with us. We have meditations for the beginning and end of the day, those for the especially wet days and some that you can try in a group of your own. We have even included a couple of our own Yoga Nidra scripts that we use and will explain a little more about them later.

All of our meditations will start with a short breathing exercise. This will be detailed at the beginning of the meditation chapters. Learn this short exercise and use it at any time when the world feels like too much.

In addition, all of these mediations can be enjoyed outdoors in a natural setting of your choice or from the comfort of your home, perhaps with natural sounds coming through your window or through the use of technology to provide natural sounds to help transport your mind to natural places.

For now, find yourself a comfortable place to sit and relax as you are guided through an amazing journey in nature. Feel connected, feel alive and most all feel at one with the natural world that surrounds us.

Meditation Tips:

Breathing rate

Breathing naturally and regularly during your meditation practice will allow your body to relax and your mind to follow the journey our meditations take you on. We always recommend taking some grounding, deep, long breaths before you start, ideally five deep breaths in through the nose if possible, and five long slow outbreaths through the mouth. Next, allowing your body to relax into its usual breathing rate.

Position

The position in which you choose to meditate is entirely personal to you. If you choose to lie down that is up to you. Please just ensure that you can maintain the position comfortably for an extended period of time.

Monkey Mind/Unwanted thoughts

We all get distracting thoughts. If these appear during your meditation practice, then acknowledge them and let them pass on by. Do not spend any time thinking on them, bring your mind back to the mediation you are currently practicing. It can help to say in our mind, "I notice you, but right now, I just need to breathe".

Temperature

The temperature that you meditate in must be comfortable and not distracting. You don't want it to be too hot or too cold (although we regularly meditate in the woods during winter). Ensuring that you are the most comfortable you can be in key.

Surroundings

When choosing the surroundings in which you meditate, you must ensure that you have as little external distraction as possible. Choose a quiet area of the home or garden or even take yourself off into nature for a real connection experience.

Routine

As with everything, initiating a routine for your meditation will enhance the effect and improve the benefits. If you meditate at the same time, in the same place and with the same intentions, it will be a more successful and enjoyable practice.

No such thing as failure

We have met so many people who say "I'm just not good at meditating". We say, you just have to keep at it and not beat yourself up if you get distracted. The act of distraction itself means that you were, even if just for a moment, meditating. Like all new skills, it takes practice. Maintain your routine and you will find your ability to focus, and concentrate will extend. There is no such thing as failing at meditating. We can all do it, we just have to find a way that works for us.

Meditation Beginning

Find yourself a comfortable position, seated on a chair or on the ground or lying down if you prefer. Rather than enforcing you sit in a particular position, or you have your eyes half closed, we prefer for you to find what is right for you with your seating/lying position and you decide if you prefer your eyes closed or open. This is your time to relax and so you know what is most comfortable for you.

Begin by taking five deep breaths in and out, breathing in through the nose if you can and slowly out through the mouth. Count slowly to five as you breathe in and count to five as you breathe out and start to bring awareness to your breath.

Now continue to breathe, becoming aware of the sensation as the air enters through the nose, touches the back of the throat, enters your lungs. Notice how your lungs inflate as you breathe in, how your back and chest move apart, and your diaphragm and belly move in order to accommodate as much air possible. Imagine yourself inflating like a balloon on each inbreath, and the change as it exits through the mouth on each outbreath.

On every outbreath, notice how your belly flattens and your diaphragm returns to neutral, how your chest and back move closer together. Notice how your ribs and intercostal muscles relax and loosen and how the warm breath leaves your mouth.

Let all thoughts slip away like the melting of ice as the sun shines on it and relax the mind. If you have a particularly busy mind, then see thoughts and noise disturbances as reminders that you are alive. Notice any thoughts or distractions by using the internal dialogue of, "I notice you, but right now, I just need to breathe" and gently guide your attention back to the breath.

Imagine as you breathe out, that you are releasing your stress, anxiety, distracting thoughts into the air. Assign a colour to them if you wish.

If you are able to mediate out in nature, then remind yourself with every inbreath you are taking in oxygen which the plants and trees provide to you and with every outbreath, you are giving back to nature with the release of carbon dioxide on your breath – you are in a symbiotic relationship with nature.

Once you have emptied your mind, allow a warm white light to flood your body and mind. This light is your power, your strength and what will support you as you continue this meditation practice.

Meditations for Morning

Morning meditation sessions were the first sessions we started running in late 2020. They have been a great experience for everyone attending and have resulted in some fantastic outcomes.

Whether you bring nature into the home or are able to enjoy meditating in an outdoor setting, morning meditations are the perfect way to start the day.

They can provide a lift in spirit and mood, as well as provide an increase in energy and zest for life to begin the day.

Equally, if you have a long or stressful day ahead, morning mediations can provide the grounding and level-headed start you might desire, providing peace and tranquility, a sense of stability and centering in a hectic world.

Morning mediations can allow you a sense of clarity and vision, which can be carried throughout your day, enabling you to make the most out of every moment and make clear, thoughtful decisions, rather than acting out of stress or worry.

Whichever way you wish to start your day, making morning meditation a part of your daily routine will help to lower heart rate, blood pressure and increase productivity and resilience.

So, what are you waiting for: wake up, stretch, breathe, and meditate.

Namaste

Sunrise Meditation

Concentrate on the breath – a five second, (or whatever is comfortable for you) long deep in breath and five seconds out breath.

Notice smells, sensations, sounds and feeling of being outdoors.

Feel the cold air through your nose and the warm breath leave your body.

Feel your ribs open up and your back and chest move away from each other as you fill your lungs with air, clean fresh woodland air. Feel the air go into your stomach, into your chest and even into your head as you breathe in deeply and slowly.

Take time to really feel connected to nature around you. As you breathe in deeply, take in all the sensations you can sense from the environment around you.

As you breathe out, feel the air leave your body and your body and muscles relax.

If you are distracted, just focus on the breath and how it feels as it enters through your nose and leaves through your mouth.

Notice the breeze on your face, the smells of the autumn leaves on the ground, the soil and mud around you and the woody smell of the trees, damp from the rain and morning dew.

Notice the bird song, the rustling of leaves as nature begins its day around you, the sounds of acorns and leaves falling around you and the breeze gently blowing in the treetops.

Feel your back relaxing as your spine lengthens and the muscles relax. Feel the tension leaving your body as you admire the scenery around you.

Your legs and lower body relax as well, feeling free and relaxed.

Really tune in to the sounds of nature and imagine the smells and sensations we usually feel in our woodland meditation space or any wooded space you feel comfortable in.

Take time to notice how still your body is and how much quieter your mind has become. Notice the stillness within and outside of your body.

Now take five deep breaths, in for five seconds and out for five seconds or longer if you can.

As you sit in your woodland space, you can view yourself either as you are sitting or from afar.

As you breathe in, the sun is just beginning to rise behind you and whether you are sat, standing, or lying down, the sun is slowly beginning to rise behand you. You can just feel the sun on the lower part of your back or at your feet if you are standing or laying down. Now with each inbreath, imagine the sun slowly rising, ever so slowly up your body, creeping gently up, spreading its warmth and energy.

As the sun rises very slowly behind you, you can see the light beginning to break through the trees around you, forming shards of golden light on the woodland floor, illuminating the golden autumn leaves around you. You can see the shadows of the tall trees around you and can feel the warmth slowly spread through your body as the sun rises further.

The sun is now halfway up your body, and the woodland floor is coming more to life around you, glowing ever more golden as the red, orange and yellow sunrise shines through the trees. As the sun slowly creeps further up your body, it finally reaches the tops of your shoulders, base of your neck and finally your head.

The light around you is brighter now and you feel warm, still, strong and full of energy to face the day.

With every inbreath, really feel that sunlight warm and energise you. If you feel you want to, you can slowly stand up in your mind and stretch, reach out to greet the day. Take in the sun's energy with every inbreath and with every outbreath, feel strong, warm, still and content.

Breathe really deeply.

When you are ready to leave this peaceful place, slowly begin to reawaken your body.

Know that you can return to this sunrise visualisation in your imagination whenever you like.

As you reawaken, keep with you the feeling of calm, peace, and relaxation.

Wiggle your fingers and toes to wake up your muscles. Shrug your shoulders. Stretch if you want to.

When you are ready, take five deep breaths and open your eyes, returning to full wakefulness, feeling alert and refreshed.

A Walk in the Forest

Imagine yourself walking on a path through a woodland. The path is soft beneath your shoes, a mixture of soil, fallen leaves, pine needles, and moss. As you walk, your body relaxes and your mind clears, more and more with each step you take.

Breathe in the fresh woodland air, filling your lungs completely with fresh oxygen that the trees give to you. Now exhale. Breathe out all the air, giving back carbon dioxide to the trees around you – a symbiotic relationship. Feeling refreshed. Take another deep breath in for five seconds.... and breathe out and out for five seconds, or three if it's more comfortable, completely letting your body relax further.

Continue to breathe slowly and deeply as you walk through the forest and continue the forest visualisation.

The air is cool, but comfortable. Sun begins to filter through the trees, making a moving dappled pattern on the ground before you, shadows of trees forming on the ground around you.

Listen to the sounds of the forest.... Birds singing. A gentle breeze blowing. The leaves on the trees shift and sway in the soft wind.

Your body relaxes more and more as you walk. Count your steps and breathe in unison with your strides. Breathe in two, three, four... hold two, three...exhale two, three, four, five.

Breathe in two, three, four... hold two, three...exhale two, three, four, five.
Breathe in two, three, four... hold two, three...exhale two, three, four, five.
Continue to breathe like this, slowly and deeply, as you become more and more relaxed.

As you walk through the forest, feel your muscles relaxing and lengthening. As your arms swing in rhythm with your walking, they become loose, relaxed, and limp.

Feel your back relaxing as your spine lengthens and the muscles relax. Feel the tension leaving your body as you admire the scenery around you.

Your legs and lower body relax as well, feeling free and relaxed. You slowly remove your shoes and socks to feel the muddy, damp, woodland floor beneath your feet. The smooth twigs, soft mud and damp gentle leaves under your feet.

As you continue to walk through the forest, you begin to explore a path, covered in soft leaves. You easily tread along smooth rocks you encounter on the path. Feeling at one with nature.

The breeze continues to blow through the treetops, but you are sheltered on the path, and the air around you is calm and still. Small saplings grow at the sides of the path. Around you is an immense array of colours. Oranges, yellows, browns, golds, all gently moving in the breeze as the sunlight touches them.

Tall trees grow on either side of the path. Picture the variety of trees around you. Some have smooth bark, others are darker, with coarse, heavy bark, deeply grooved.

You stop along your walk to touch the bark of the large tree next to you. It is a tree you have met before; it feels familiar to you, and you feel strength when you place your full palm on the tree trunk. Breathe deeply in and relax completely as you breathe out.

Smell the forest around you. The air is fresh, and filled with the scent of trees, soil, leaves and life.

Continue to enjoy the woodland around you. Take some nice deep breaths and take time to look around your woodland.

Feel the sun, warm on your skin. Feel the gentle breeze blow across your cheek. Listen to the birds singing. The leaves rustling in the breeze. Squirrels chattering.

Breathe really deeply and slowly.

When you are ready to leave this peaceful place, slowly begin to reawaken your body. Know that you can return to this forest visualisation in your imagination whenever you like.

As you reawaken, keep with you the feeling of calm, peace, and relaxation. Wiggle your fingers and toes to wake up your muscles. Shrug your shoulders. Stretch if you want to.

When you are ready, open your eyes and return to full wakefulness, feeling alert and refreshed.

Worry Stone

Hold a large stone in your hand, a stone that fits in the palm of your hand and feels satisfying to touch.

Concentrate on the breath – five seconds long, deep inbreath and a five second, slow out breath.

Notice smells, sensations, sounds and feeling of being outdoors.

Feel the cold air through your nose and the warm breath leave your body. Feel your ribs open up and your back and chest move away from each other as you fill your lungs with air, clean fresh woodland air. Feel the air go into your stomach, into your chest and even into your head as you breathe in deeply and slowly.

Take time to really feel connected to nature around you. As you breathe in deeply, take in all the sensations you can sense from the environment around you.

As you breathe out, feel the air leave your body and you feel every fibre of your body relax and let go.

If you are distracted, just focus on the breath and how it feels as it enters through your nose and leaves through your mouth.

Notice the breeze on your face, the smells of the autumn leaves on the ground, the soil and mud around you and the woody smell of the trees, damp from the rain and morning dew.

Notice the bird song, the rustling of leaves as nature begins its day around you, the sounds of acorns and leaves falling around you and the breeze gently blowing in the treetops.

Now, as you breathe in, imagine a light begins to fill your body on each inbreath and the light fades on every outbreath. Breath in and you begin to fill with the morning sunlight, breath out and the light fades.

Feel light and warmth within your body as the light spreads throughout your body, filling you with its energy, warmth and hope of a new day.

Notice how still you are, how calm you are, how warm and full of light and hope you are.

Take a moment to feel completely still within. Enjoy the light and warmth that fills you and relax as you breathe out and the light fades. Notice the stone in your hand as you relax. Notice the temperature of the stone, the shape and texture under your skin.

Now, slowly draw your attention to a worry, anxiety or stress you have, but do not dwell on it. Sit with the feeling this worry or stress brings to you. Sitting with uncomfortable thoughts and feelings is difficult but builds resilience and removes the power of such negative experiences.

On each inbreath fill your body with light, warmth and hope and on each outbreath, push the light down your arm and squeeze your worry, anxiety or stress into your stone.

Breath in and feel light fill your body, breathe out and push your worry or stress, along with the light, down your shoulder, along your arm, into your hand, through your fingertips and into the stone.

Visualise the worry or stress rushing down your arm as a flash of light, leaving your shoulder, arm, hand and fingertips and entering into the stone.

Focus that light, warmth and energy rushing from your body, down your arm, into your hand and into the stone, taking your worries with it.

Really push those worries into the stone. Feel them leaving your body, focus on the light re-filling your body with each inbreath and releases the anxiety, tension and stress on each outbreath and into the stone.

Notice the warmth of the stone as it fills with energy, negative energy taken from your mind, through your body, down your shoulder, your arm, your hand and into the stone. You may experience warmth, tingling and strong waves of emotion – this is completely normal and ok.

Breathe deeply. You are strong. You've got this. You can begin your day afresh, energised and with any anxiety contained and manageable in your stone.

Loosen your grip on your stone if you have a tight grip, notice how you feel the desire to let your stone go, to let it fall from your fingers and to release your tension. Some people feel the need to throw their stone far away from them and others wish to carry the stone with them – either is ok, do what feels right for you.

Take five nice deep breaths and when you are ready to leave this peaceful place, slowly begin to reawaken your body. As you reawaken, keep with you the feeling of calm, peace, and relaxation. If you wish to, take your stone with you or simply let it go, let it drop and leave your worries behind.

Flight with Birds

Concentrate on the breath – breathing in for five seconds or longer if possible. And exhale for five seconds or longer.

Notice smells, sensations, sounds and feeling of being outdoors.

Feel the cold air through your nose and the warm breath leave your body.

Feel your ribs open up and your back and chest move away from each other as you fill your lungs with air, clean fresh woodland air. Feel the air go into your stomach, into your chest and even into your head as you breathe in deeply and slowly.

Take time to really feel connected to nature around you. As you breathe in deeply, take in all the sensations you can sense from the environment around you. As you breathe out, feel the air leave your body and your body and muscles relax.

If you are distracted, just focus on the breath and how it feels as it enters through your nose and leaves through your mouth. Notice the breeze on your face, the smells of the leaves around you, the soil and mud and the woody smell of the trees, damp from the rain and morning dew.

Notice the bird song, the rustling of leaves as nature begins its day around you, the sounds of acorns and leaves falling around you and the breeze gently blowing in the treetops.

Really tune in to bird sound if you can hear it, if you cannot hear birds clearly, use your memory and your mind, you can recall the sounds you have heard in earlier mediations or memories you have of other bird sounds.

Visualise yourself walking through the woodland along a never-ending woodland path and as you walk slowly and softly, you can hear lots of bird sounds. Take three deep breaths, taking in all the sights, sounds and sensations nature has to offer you.

Notice that on each inbreath, the bird song is getting louder and louder and on each outbreath the sound fades away. Feel your belly, chest, lungs and head fill with oxygen and fresh air from nature as you breath in deeply. On each outbreath, feel relaxed and ready to explore your woodland further.

As you breathe deeper and deeper, each inbreath makes you feel stronger and bigger, more confident. Feel your chest and lungs expand and your shoulders broaden as you walk through your woodland. As you take deep breaths, the bird song becomes louder around you and you feel like you can lift slightly off the ground with each step forward. You feel light and strong on each in breath, with a bounce in your step and outbreath.

You begin to quicken the pace of your walk and feel yourself feeling lighter and lighter. Your pace has now quickened to a gentle jog and each time your feet land on the ground, you bounce slightly upwards, to a point where you feel that if you leapt you might just fly.

Really focus on the bird song and the feeling of strength as you breathe in deep into your chest and feel your shoulders get broader and stronger.

Now as you gain momentum and you feel lighter and lighter on each step, you begin to leap slightly and float for a short time between each step. Now as you breathe in the deepest you can, you feel wings release from your shoulder blades and as you leap up towards the sky, you begin to flap your wings and gain height to the top of the tree canopy.

Now on each inbreath, you have to flap really hard to maintain your flight and on each out breath you soar without the need to flap.

On each inbreath, imagine more and more birds surround you, coming closer to you and you must flap hard to keep up.
Also, each outbreath, the birds disperse away from you, but remain in view and you sore without needing to flap so hard to keep up.

Breathe in and the birds move in close as you flap harder.
Breathe out and the birds move away, but in view and you soar.

Now as you breathe in, there are more and more birds around you, but you no longer need to flap so hard to keep up, you are right in the middle of the flock and can glide on the sir currents the other birds create around you.

As you exhale, you soar forward ahead of the flock as they spread out all around you. Still in view and there if you need them, but you soar forward with ease, strength and confidence. Inhale and your flock return to you, exhale and you soar ahead with ease, with power.

Your flock remain in sight and are there if you need them, but now as you breath in, they no longer need to move in close to you to support you. You've got this all by yourself and as you breathe in and out, flying is easy and you sore high, fast, with confidence, surrounded by support if you need it, but you're ok, you've got this.

Breath in deeply as you flap gently and breathe out, fully exhale as you propel forward, soaring in the sky. Enjoy the view around you whether it's mountains, woodland treetops, the sea……. enjoy your view, knowing you can do this. Spend the next few moments enjoying flying, feeling free and full of hope.

Take time in the meditation to soar for as long as you need.

Now it is time to return to the woodland where you first started your journey. You may find it difficult to land your bird and you may wish to stay a little longer soaring high – that's absolutely fine. Take your time, there is no rush.

As you fly in the sky over fields, mountains, sea and woodland, you make your way back towards the tree canopy of the woodland where you started your journey. Knowing that as you reach the tree canopy you will be able to gently glide all the way back through the trees to land back on the woodland path on your feet, with ease and grace.

You feel your feet steady and sure on the woodland path and continue to walk all the way back to where you started your woodland journey. Back past the trees and wildflowers, surrounded by bird song, surrounded by nature. Until you are all the way back where you started, in the middle of the woodland and knowing you can always return whenever you need to fly once more, to feel light, to feel free, to feel full of hope.

Know that you can return to this bird visualisation in your imagination whenever you like, then take 5 deep breaths and you can open your eyes.

A meditation for letting go.

Imagine yourself standing in a lush green field at the start of a trail that winds to a path into a forest. Take a step onto the trail and head off into the forest. As you walk down the path, you notice how the sun kisses your face, and you hear the birdsong echoing in the trees. You smell the scent of pine needles and the cool, fresh air. You feel how a breeze lightly ruffles your hair. You notice the fallen pine needles carpeting the path, making a soft and cushioned surface on which you walk. You feel a deep sense of peace and connection to the forest and all of your surroundings.

You feel safe, you feel at peace, and you feel at home.

Gradually, you begin to hear the sound of rushing water. Just up ahead you see the sunlight glinting off the water, and your path takes you in that direction. You come to the bank of a babbling brook, with the rushing water cascading over rocks, revealing a sandy bottom.

You can see there are three steps in the bank which lead you down to water. When you reach the steps, you take a deep breath in and as you breathe out, you step down the steps, sitting on the bottom step.

You sit and rest for a while. You take off your shoes and socks and let your toes and feet dip into the cool water, noticing how good it feels as the cool, smooth water rushing over your skin. You see wildflowers and grass growing by the banks, and you become aware of the many different colours in the flowers that contrast and complement each other. You observe how the water has worn smooth the river rocks. You can smell the fresh water intermingled with the smell of the grass and the wildflowers that surround you.

From where you sit, you notice that the middle of the brook is where the water flows fastest, obscuring the bottom as well as anything in the water. But by the side of the bank are protected pools, where the water is still, and you can see very clearly their contents, from the sandy bottom to the frogs and fish that reside there. Those still pools are similar to your mind while you are meditating—slowing down and stilling the mind allows you to examine what it contains, mindfully noting what it reveals, and pondering it without judgment. The fast-moving water is like our mind on some days—with our thoughts moving so quickly that we cannot see what lies beneath. We cannot sit with our emotions, nor can we be mindful of them.

You turn your head to look upstream and can see all the water that soon will flow past you, just like all the breaths you still will take, adventures still to be experienced, and days yet to be lived. As you look downstream, you see all of the water that has already flowed by this spot, similar to the breaths you have already taken, memories already experienced, days that have been lived.

Just as you cannot control the water upstream that will flow past you, you also cannot call back the water that has already passed. All you can do is live in the present moment, noting what it holds. You cannot live in the past, though some might dwell on it. Similarly, you can't speed up the future, though often you might try to control or manipulate it. It is best to embrace the scene just in front of you—the water and sensations that appear at your particular point on the riverbank, noting and appreciating these present moments for what they offer.

Taking in one more breath of the fresh river air, you put on your shoes and socks, stand up, and head back down the path the way that you came. As you head back into the forest you note the play of light piercing through the forest canopy. You observe the different shades of green in the pine needles, the plant leaves, and the moss growing on rocks and trees. You note the texture of different rocks, leaves, and bark under your fingers.

Now you are back at the trailhead, and you step again into the field of your daily life. Note how mindful you were in the transitions from field to forest to brook and back again and resolve to be aware in your everyday transitions. Take a few moments in the field to begin bringing awareness back into the body, wiggling fingers and toes and moving your hands and feet. You know that you can return to the river or the forest in your mind anytime you need to drop into peace, tranquility, and comfort.

Take a few mindful breaths and open your eyes to conclude the meditation.

Meditations for Evening

There is something magical about a woodland in the evening. Whether early evening and you can observe the sun setting through the trees, casting shards of beautiful coloured light through the levels of the woodlands or the all-encompassing darkness of the woodland with the stars and the moon, to illuminate the way. Woodlands or outdoor spaces at night are beautiful and can provide a real sense of solitude and belonging.

In the beautiful woodland setting we are lucky enough to inhabit for many evenings throughout the year, we use fairy lights around our meditation space to provide a sense of warmth and safety, especially in the darker and cooler winter months. Sitting there, in the darkness of nature, surrounded by the creaking and popping of the bark on the trees as the temperature drops and the bark shrinks back to the tree.

Hearing the sound of owls communicating clearly to each other across the natural landscape, small mammals moving around in the undergrowth and if we are lucky enough, the presence of a deer visits us as we remain still and a part of the magic.

Sitting in your garden as the sun drops behind the horizon and as the nocturnal world comes alive, is just as awe-inspiring and connective as being in a woodland.

Evening meditates offer a complete stillness and serenity, which perhaps you have sought all day. Make time in an evening for your brain to file and process everything it needs to during your mediations and experience the best sleep of your life!

Woodland Canopy

Begin, as we always encourage you to do, by taking five deep breaths. In through the nose for five seconds if possible and out through the mouth, again for five seconds or longer.

Noticing on each inbreath as your chest and belly inflate, like a balloon. Imagine the fresh oxygen in each breath filling your body, even your head. And on each outbreath, allowing the breath to take with it and stress and pain, feeling your body relax to neutral as you exhale.

As you continue to breathe in this way, in through the nose, if possible, and out through the mouth, long slow breaths, imagine yourself, if you can, in a woodland at night.

You are surrounded by trees and the moon in the sky illuminates the woodland floor in front of you, as bright as a torch and allows you to see all the different sizes and shapes of trees around you, in silhouette.

Directly above you, where the moonlight pierces through a gap in the tree canopy above, you can see a beautiful clear starry sky. Still and soothing and clear, allowing your mind to feel still, calm and clear too.

You take a deep breath in and absorb the beautiful stillness that surrounds you and as you breathe out you feel yourself soothed and relaxed by the moonlit woodlands. You feel warmth and safe and completely at peace.

As you stand there, in the woodland, lit by the bright moon above and the starry sky, you hear the movement of woodland animals around you. Badgers and foxes snuffle around in the undergrowth, awakening from their slumber and beginning to search for food as their shift in the woodland begins. You may hear and see deer, bravely venturing out in the peaceful, still solace both you and they find in the woodland at nighttime. You hear an owl hotting somewhere nearby and a second return it's call.

You take three deep breaths, as you allow your sense to flood with all that nature has to offer you, the smell of the damp woodland floor beneath your feet, the sounds of the nocturnal woodland and the sensations all around you. And on the third breath, as you exhale, your gaze falls upon a large tree, which appears to be completely illuminated by moonlight.

The tree calls you, pulls you and as you stand there in awe of the moonlit tree, you see a spiral staircase form around the trunk of this majestic tree. The staircase can be metal or wooden and winds its way all the way from the base of the trunk to the above the tree canopy and out of site, as your eyes trace up the tree.

You know that you must climb the tree and on taking another deep breath in and breath out, you make your way towards the bottom step of the spiral staircase. You know the staircase and the tree will guide you, keep you safe and lead you where it is you need to be.

Take a deep breath in once more, and as you breathe out, begin to climb the spiral staircase. Breath by breath, step by step, working your way further up the tree, slowly and surely, with confidence and hope in your heart.

As you begin to near the top of the tree, you find the spiral staircase weaves its way through the tree canopy, past leaves, branches and twigs, until you find yourself at the top of the tree, where the staircase ends, and you appear on top of a wooden platform.

The platform is strong and sturdy, and you know you are safe and held, supported, and encouraged by the strength of the tree. And from the platform, you see the most beautiful view and sky you have ever seen. There may be valleys and mountains, or fields and villages, perhaps rivers and rocks, all illuminated by the moonlight.

You take a seat on the wooden platform and stop to notice just how many stars fill the night sky. You feel safe and warm and held. You take a deep breath in and clench one of your fists and you breath out, keeping the fist clenched. On your next inbreath, bring to mind a worry or pain, struggle or strain which ways you down, a trouble you carry with you.

Allow yourself a few more deep breaths in and out as you sit with the uncomfortable feeling this worry or stress gives you, noticing where in your body you most feel the tension this weight your bear causes you. Perhaps a tightness in the chest, butterflies in the stomach, a prickly sensation on the back of the neck. Know that as you sit there with this uncomfortable sensation and thought, that you are supported by the tree beneath you.

Know that nature can carry this burden for you and that in a few moments you will allow yourself to let go of whatever it is that holds you back. Know that you are strong, courageous, and wonderful and that you will get through whatever it is that holds you back and weighs you down.

You raise your clenched fist so that is in front of you, and you open your fist and find a ball of orange or yellow light, an orb floating in the centre of your palm. This orb of light is your worry or stress, pain or difficulty which you carry with you and which you are about to be free of.

Take a deep breath in and as you breathe out, you allow your outbreath to blow the orb of light away from the palm of your hand and towards the night sky. Initially, it may be difficult to get the orb to move away from your hand, or perhaps it moves away with ease, but with each outbreath you take, you are able to blow the orb further and further into the night sky, until your orb vanishes into the distance and becomes another star in the sky.

Allow yourself a moment to notice how you feel now. You may feel lighter, perhaps a tingling in your body, a sense of freedom and of hope. Although meditation cannot solve your problems, it can give you moments of stillness like this, a moment of freedom, a moment of hope, light in the darkness.

And as you sit there in the moonlight, surrounded by a stunning night view, with a sky full of stars, just notice how still you are: how still you feel both in body and mind.

You can now repeat this exercise, bringing other worries to mind, creating an orb of light as you sit there with the difficult feelings and thoughts and release yourself from them, if only for a moment, as they become stars in the night sky.

Repeat this as many times as you need and then take a moment to ensure the stillness and peace you feel.

When you are ready, it is time to return to the spiral staircase, this time taking a deep breath in and out as you descend the first step. Knowing you can always return whenever you need to feel peace and stillness and whenever you need to feel free and full of hope. To feel lighter and to find the light in the darkness, whenever you need it.

Then when you reach the bottom of the spiral staircase and find yourself back in the woodland, illuminated by moonlight, with a sky full of stars, surrounded by nature, surrounded by hope and life, then take five deep breaths and you can open your eyes.

Moonlit Pool

Seat yourself in a comfortable position and begin by taking five deep breaths, in through the nose for five seconds if possible. If you can only breathe in through your mouth, that's ok. Then release your breath slowly and for five seconds or longer.

Follow the journey of air as it enters your nose, moved to the back of your throat, down into the lungs where it inflates the lungs, causing the belly to rise and the diaphragm to move.

Noticing how your ribs expand and the muscle between them stretch on every inbreath and on every outbreath how the ribs and return to neutral and the muscle relax and slacken off, letting go of any tension and stress or strain from the day.

As you continue to breathe in this way, imagine yourself in a woodland at night. The woods are still and dark apart from the sounds of nature as it settles in for the evening and as some animals awaken.

Although the woodland is dark, the moon illuminates the woodland floor around you, highlighting the soil and roots and leaves of which it is made. As the moon shines so brightly to can see the silhouettes of the trees all around you. As you stand there in the moonlight, you feel safe and peaceful and at home, knowing the woodland will protect you and guide you through your journey.

As you remain standing in the centre of your woodland, lit by the moonlight, you hear small mammals moving around in the undergrowth and perhaps the sound of owls communicating with each other. The nocturnal animals trust you and know they are safe to show themselves in your presence. You may see deer, foxes, bats or badgers; all happy for you to share their woodland with them.

You take a deep breath in, allowing nature to fill your senses and as you breathe out, you notice a path ahead of you, which will lead you deeper into the woodland and you can see from where you stand that the path leads gently downhill.

You take another deep breath in and as you breathe out, you begin to walk along the woodland path, the gently sloping downhill woodland path. You can feel the ground come up to meet your feet with every step; sure, and constant, the moonlight guides you with every step.

As the path slopes further downhill, leading you deeper into the woods, the light continues to shine brightly down in front of you, allowing you're every step to be safe and sure. As the woods grow denser, the trees hug closer to you, and you pass close to animals which trust you to share the woodland with them. You smell scents of the damp woodland floor with its leaves and soil and roots, as well as the earthy scent of mosses and fears which are scattered around the woodland.

Eventually, up ahead, you can see that the woodland path comes to an end. There is an arch in the trees where the path leads you out to a clearing. In the clearing the moon shines down ever brighter and in front of you is a beautiful moonlit pool of water. The pool of water is surrounded by rocks, to which there are three steps at the front edge nearest to you, which acts as a way to enter the pool of water.

You take a deep breath in and as you breathe out, just notice how still you are, how calm and at peace you feel on the edge of the woodland, in the clearing, by the moonlit pool, illuminate by light that reflects on the still, black surface of the water.

Take another deep inhale and as you exhale, move towards the three steps which lead up to the moonlit pool and notice how the water gently steams in the cool night air. You know without even touching the moonlit pool that the water is warm and welcoming, like a soothing bath.

At this point you sit down on the edge of the rocks at the top of the three steps and you can choose to remove you shoes and socks and dip your feet in to the beautifully warming and calming water or you can allow yourself to enter the water fully, knowing you are safe and will be held and supporting by the warm water.

Whether you choose to dip your feet, or to fully immerse yourself in the moonlit pool, as soon as the warm smooth water touches your skin, you are warmed throughout your whole body. You feel the warm water of the pool relieve any aches or pains and melt away stress or tension. You may choose to lie on your back and float in the warm pool, allowing your whole body to be supported and for the water to take the weight or your body and any aches, stress or worries you carry with you.

You take a moment to allow yourself complete stillness as you look at the most beautiful starry sky you have ever seen, with the moon illuminating the secret pool you have found in the clearing at the edge of the deepest part of your woodland.

You feel supported, you feel every muscle let go and you feel loved. The moonlit pool cleanses your body and mind, soothes you and hugs you, reminding you, you are special, you are wonderful, and you are welcome here any time. Spend the next few moments for you; enjoying the feeling of the warm water on your skin, the freshness of the night air and the connection you have with nature.

When you are ready, knowing you can always return to the moonlit pool, whenever you need to feel held, loved and a moment of complete stillness and peace; it is time to leave the pool, knowing you will be completely dry and warm as soon as you step out.

You take a deep breath in and out as you enjoy the clearing one last time and you make your way back towards the arch in the trees at the edge of the woodland, which leads you back to the path. The path, which this time has a gentle incline. The path is easy to walk, nothing too strenuous and you know the moonlight will guide back up the path to exactly where you started.

Along the return journey, you pass the earthy scent of ferns and mosses, the smell of the damp woodland floor and the sounds of the animals nearby who trust you enough to show themselves to you. Perhaps you hear the owls again as you continue to make your way back to where you started. Perhaps you see deer moving around in the distance, who stop to make eye contact with you as you pass by.

You eventually find yourself back where you started your journey; in the woodland at night, with the moon illuminating your woodland floor in front of you. Surrounded by trees, surrounded by nature.

And knowing you can always find your way back to the moonlit pool whenever you need to, then when you are ready, just take five deep breaths and open your eyes.

The Northern Lights

Begin, as we always encourage you to do, by taking five deep breaths. In through the nose for five seconds if possible and out through the mouth, again for five seconds or longer.

Noticing on each inbreath as your chest and belly inflate, like a balloon. Imagine the fresh oxygen in each breath filling your body, even your head. And on each outbreath, allowing the breath to take with it and stress and pain, feeling your body relax to neutral as you exhale.

As you continue to breathe in this way, in through the nose, if possible, and out through the mouth, long slow breaths, imagine yourself, if you can, in a woodland at night.

You are surrounded by trees and the moon in the sky illuminates the woodland floor in front of you, as bright as a torch and allows you to see all the different sizes and shapes of trees around you, in silhouette. Directly above you, where the moonlight pierces through a gap in the tree canopy above, you can see a beautiful clear starry sky. Still and soothing and clear, allowing your mind to feel still, calm and clear too.

You take a deep breath in and absorb the beautiful stillness that surrounds you and as you breathe out you feel yourself soothed and relaxed by the moonlit woodlands. You feel warmth and safe and completely at peace.

As you stand there in the woodlands, illuminated by moonlight, you know that the wildlife within the woodland is close by and welcome your presence. You may hear the sound of the Tawny owls hooting to each other, or perhaps the snuffling in the undergrowth of a badger or fox, as well as the tiny shuffles and scuffles of the small mammals which inhabit your woodland and are secretly darting around in the ivy, ferns and wildflowers which cover the edges of the woodland floors. You know that the animals which live within your woodland trust you and you can trust them, to keep you safe, to guide you and to always welcome you into nature.

You take three deep breaths, and on each breath, you absorb all the sights, sounds and sensations that nature has to offer you in the woodland at night. On the third breath as you exhale, you see a path has appeared in front of you. A path which can, as always, be winding or straight, laid with soils and leaves and roots, or perhaps laid with pine needles and stones. Whatever you see if absolutely fine. This is your woodland, and you know the path which you see before will guide you to wherever you need to be.

The moonlight illuminates the woodland path which has appeared to you, and you can see that the path gently slopes downhill into deeper part of the woodland. Taking another deep breath in and knowing you will be guided by the moonlight and by nature every step you take, as you breathe out, you begin to walk the woodland path.

Step by step and breath by breath, you feel the ground come up to meet your feet and you continue to follow the path, gently sloping downhill, deeper and deeper into the woodland. You know and feel with every step that you are safe; you feel an energy or excitement as to where this path will lead you too and above all you feel at home.

In the moonlight, you can make out the shapes of trees and plants around you, you can smell the dampness of this deeper part of the woodland, your woodland.

Eventually, up ahead, you can see that the path begins to level out and the trees make an archway where the woodland comes to an end and to enter a new area of your woodland.

As you reach the archway the trees have made for you, you find yourself leaving the woodland and stepping on to a rocky, pebbly shoreline. You find yourself at the edge of a large loch or lake, surrounded by mountains and with a dark, dark sky above you, decorated with stars as far as you can see and the light of the beautiful moon still guiding you.

You take a deep breath in, and as you breathe out, you make your way down the cobbled shore until you are stood at the end of the waterline, looking across the large lock or lake, which is completely still and appears black due to the darkness of the night sky.

As you stand there, guided by the moon and the stars above you, looking across the beautifully still and serene lake, just notice how still you are. How still you feel in your body and your mind and just how peaceful and magical this place feels. Know in this moment, just how lucky you are that your connection with nature has guided you here and the loch has revealed itself to you, because you are wonderful and peaceful and above all, connected with nature.

As you stand and enjoy the stars and moon reflected in the loch or lake in front of you, you can see a faint mist appear just above the surface of the water, showing you that the water in the loch is warm and welcoming.

You notice, as you stand there admiring the stillness and the depth of the lake as the moon and stars reflect upon its serene surface, that colours begin to appear from within the water. Flashes of green and blue, perhaps yellow, orange, and pink. The water in front of you begins to come alive with a firework display of colours from the depths of the loch water itself. The water is alive with colour created by the bioluminescent life within the loch, created by organisms as they move and connect, displaying all their beauty to you and inviting you into the water.

At this point, you have a choice, you can choose to remain on the shoreline of the loch or lake, admiring the beautiful display of colour within the water, or you can choose to take a deep breath in and as you breathe out, step in to the lake, knowing you are safe and can maintain contact with the bottom of the lake with every step should you need to.

The water is warm like a soothing and relaxing bath; easing aches and pains and allowing you to let go of stresses and strains you may carry with you. The water surrounds you and you feel free and alive, your body held and supported by the water of the gloriously warm water, alive with colours and lights. You are safe, you are warm, and you are completely free.

You may choose you lie on our back and allow the warm lake water to take the strain and lift you, so you float effortlessly; all the time surrounded in the water by energy, life and light, as the colours continue to cascade in the water around you, ever stronger with blues and greens and yellows. Just spend the next few moments for you, floating on the surface of the warm and colourful lake, admiring the stars in the night sky and the moonlight, feeling complete peace and quiet, yet energy and life at the same time. You may feel tingling or a warmth or a sense of hope and excitement race through your body.

You may see the odd shooting star race across the night sky as you take time for you, to feel held, to feel loved and to feel connected with nature. As you lie there in the lake, held, and supported, surrounded by the still, warm water with the bioluminescent lights all around you, you notice the same colours appearing in the night sky. Flashes of blue, green, yellow, orange, and pink lights in the night sky.

You take a deep breath in and out as you enjoy the display of colours you see in the night sky. Colours which resemble the northern lights, colours which surround you in the water. At this point, it is impossible to tell whether the colours which represent life and energy in the water which supports and holds you, are reflected in the night sky or whether the northern lights display in the sky are not reflected in the water.

It is almost as if the night sky and the lake have become one and you are in the centre of it all, flooded with energy, hope and freedom from the warm water that surrounds you and a sense of joy, excitement, and energy from the lights in the sky high above you.

Send the next few minutes enjoying being suspended between water and air as your body tingles and senses the energy and warmth of this beautiful display of colour and love that nature has shown you tonight. In this moment, know just how lucky you are, how privileged you are that the nature, and the universe has shown itself to you, and only you, in all its power and glory. It is not unusual to feel tingling, warmth, a sense of energy flowing through your body. It is also not unusual to feel lightheaded in this moment of complete connection with the natural world.

Before too long, the night sky light display begins to fade, until the sky is dark once more apart from stars and the moon, which remains bright. The water around you too becomes dark once more and still, with all the lights fading away.

You make your way to the shoreline and step onto the cobbled shore, knowing you will be instantly dry and warm and knowing you will carry the energy and warmth with you as you take a last look at the serene stillness of the black lake and the starry sky above you.

Meditations for Wet Weather

There is nothing more invigorating or refreshing than meditating in the rain, especially when you are surrounded by trees and can hear the raindrops as they reach differing levels of the woodland, from canopy to ground. On the whole, we are fairly lucky with the weather in the session we deliver in the woods, but on occasion we do get the odd wet weather day and encourage our wonderful participants to opt into a rain mediation and experience the sense of freedom and energy it offers. So, why not try it for yourself with our own raindrop mediation and experience feeling alive and awakened by the journey of raindrops.

The Rain Drop

Find yourself a comfortable position to sit or lie in as you prepare to experience a rain mediation. Begin by taking five deep, slow breaths. In through the nose if you are able to and out through the mouth, ideally for five seconds or longer. Imagine your body inflating like a balloon on each inbreath, and on each outbreath allow every muscle and tendon every fibre of your being to let go and loosen off.

Know with each inbreath that you are flooding your red blood cells with fresh oxygen from the trees and plants around you and that with each outbreath, you are giving back to nature with carbon dioxide. Imagine if you wish that the trees breathe in simultaneously with you and breathe out at the same time too. You are connected with nature through breathing and all you need to do right now is to continue to breathe in and out.

As you sit there, in the rain, breathing in through the nose (if you can) and out through mouth, long, slow, deep breaths, just begin to notice the sound of the raindrops around you. Can you hear the different levels of the woodlands or your surroundings as you turn your attention to listening to the raindrops. Can you hear each rain drop fall from leaf to leaf and branch to branch, until they reach the floor on which you sit?

As you sit there, with your attention tuned into the rain around you, you may hear life carrying on outside the woodland wherever you are. Perhaps cars, people dogs, these are reminder that you are alive and that whilst the rest of the world attempts to rush in and out of the rain to avoid getting wet, you sit there still, calm, peaceful, absorbing the rain into your body and mind, at one with the raindrops which surround you.

If you can in your mind, as you sit listening to the rain fall around you, imagine yourself (if you are not already) in a woodland, surrounded by trees, plants, wildflowers and life. Although the rain continues to fall around you, in your woodland you are sheltered and protected, knowing that each raindrop that reaches your skin has been sent by nature to enrich your life, to cleanse you of negative thoughts and feels and to nourish you.

You are still, you are calm, and you feel at home and soothed by the steady fall of raindrops all around you. And as you sit there, in your woodland, surrounded by nature, surrounded by life, your attention is drawn to the floor around you. You can see the indents in the soil as raindrops make it through the tree canopy above and land near to you. You can see the splash as certain raindrops fall from leaf to leaf. The rain brings freshness, energy, and hope.

You find your attention now centred on one particular tree in your woodland as the rain continues to fall steadily around you. Perhaps you are drawn to this tree as it is the largest in your woodland, or perhaps you like the colour and patterns you can see in the bark, or perhaps the shape and colour of the leaves or blossom on your tree.

Whichever the reason, you find yourself studying this tree, from the base of the trunk, all the way to its branches and leaves, and the top of the tree canopy. As you trace your eyes back down the tree, towards the base of the trunk once more, you notice that a staircase has appeared. A staircase which wraps itself all the way around your tree. A spiral staircase which begins at the base of the trunk and will lead you all the way to the top of the tree canopy.

You take a deep breath in, and as you breathe out, you begin to walk towards the bottom step of the spiral staircase. Knowing the staircase is strong and will support you and will guide you all the way from the base of the tree to the top of the canopy above, you take another deep breath in and as you breathe out, you begin to climb the staircase. Winding your way slowly around the trunk of the tree, step by step and breath by breath. You are safe, you are calm, and you feel the energy of the rain all around you. You feel alive.

Eventually you reach the top of the staircase and the top of the tree canopy, where there is a platform on which you can sit and rest. Where you can see for miles across the expanse of the woodland and where you can feel the full force of the rain as it soothes, heals and energises you each time it lands on your skin.

As you sit there, at the top of the tree, on the woodland platform at the top of the spiral staircase, you find your attention drawn to each individual raindrop as they land on the tree canopy in which you rest. It is almost as if the rain can be viewed by each individual raindrop, and you follow the journey of each drop as they cascade and trickle gently down through the leaves of the tree in which you sit.

You find yourself able to follow the journey of many individual raindrops, watching contently as they land on one of the top leaves of the tree canopy and tricky slow down onto the leaf below and the leaf below that and so on, until you can see through the leaves and see the raindrop land gently on the woodland floor beneath you.

You repeat this several times, just breathing in through the nose and out through the mouth and with your only job right now, to watch individual raindrops as they journey through the layers of the woodlands, from top to bottom of your tree.

As you sit there, full of life and energy from the rain which continues to fall around you and on you, you wonder what it might be like to be a raindrop. How it might feel to have the freedom to journey all the way from the crown of the tree to the base of the trunk, leaf by leaf, branch by branch. How it might feel to place complete trust in nature and know that the tree will guide you as you journey down through each layer of the woodland.

And now it is time for you to feel exactly what it feels like. If you can, as you watch the rain continue to fall, you follow one raindrop as it falls from the clouds and lands on a leaf in front of you and you are instantly the raindrop. You can feel yourself slide along the leaves, reaching the top of the leaf and falling ever so gently onto the leaf below. Sliding at whatever speed you choose to, leaf by leaf, making your way slowly but surely, through the layers of the woodland and the tree. At times perhaps, travelling the length of branches, enjoying the freedom and excitement you feel as you put your trust completely in nature and make your way steadily and surely all the way to the lowest leaf on the tree. At this point you trickle from the leaf, along the branch towards the trunk of the tree and where the branch meets the trunk, you then trickle down the grooves in the bark of your tree, until you find yourself at the base of the trunk, where you become yourself once more. The spiral staircase slowly disappears before your eyes.

You place your hands on the wet bark of the trunk of the tree and trace your fingers in the groove in which you just travelled as a raindrop.

You feel alive, energised and completely connected with nature. You take one last look from the base of the trunk where it meets the wet ground around you, all the way up the trunk to the branches and leaves and to top of the tree canopy above you.

And now with your feet firmly on the ground, surrounded by trees, surrounded by nature, knowing you can always return whenever you need to watch the rain and feel refreshed, complete peace and alive, then when you are ready, take five deep breaths and you can open your eyes.

Meditations for A Deeper Nature Connection

For some of us, mediation is an escapism, a way to quieten the mind and to find peace and stillness in an otherwise fast-paced and busy world. Mediation is a fantastic way to allow yourself a moment of tranquility and to enable every part of your body and mind to slow down.

Meditation can also offer a deep and spiritual experience; a chance to connect with yourself and nature on a much deeper level. When we discuss a deeper level of mediation, we are operating in a different wave patter within our brain function, a place between conscious and unconscious.

In these moments, where we may experience the drop off a cliff sensation or the feeling of falling, we can open our minds and hearts to alternative images, experiences and connections.

Spirit guides and spirit animals may appear to us in these moments when our hearts and minds are fully open. It is also possible to experience and view ancestral lives, families and faces you know you are connected to, but have never seen before.

In our woodland setting, we have been lucky enough for our regular meditators and those new to mediation to have experienced deep and meaningful connections.

Mediation is unique to every individual, and you are free to take from it whatever you like, whether meaningful and spiritual or peaceful and calming.

Spirit Animal

Begin this meditation with five deep breaths technique previously detailed in earlier meditations and at the start of the book.

Imagine yourself if you can, in a woodland bathed in sunlight. It can be a woodland you are sitting in to experience this meditation, a woodland you have visited before, or somewhere completely of your imagination.

Wherever you are, you are surrounded by trees and their leaves sway slightly in a beautiful gentle breeze which passes through the woodland. Where the breeze moves the branches and their leaves, the sunlight breaks through and shards of orange, yellow and golden light dance around on the woodland floor around you.

You take a deep breath, breathing in all the sights, sounds and sensations that nature has to offer you. You can hear various birds all around you, calling to each other, busily collecting seeds and small insects to feed their young. You may see squirrels jumping from tree to tree, free and full of energy and life. There may be rabbits, perhaps small mammals busy darting around in the undergrowth, seeking berries and seeds to store away. You may see bees and butterflies where the sunlight breaks through the tree canopy and shines upon wildflowers. You may even see deer in the distance in the woodland.

This is your woodland, and you feel safe, relaxed, and completely at ease. You take another deep breath in and as you breathe out you can see a path in the woodland ahead of you which leads deeper into the woodland. The path can be laid with soil, roots and leaves, or pine needles, or perhaps stones. Whatever you see is absolutely fine.

You begin to walk along the woodland path, noticing all the vibrant colours of your woodland. The lush green of the trees and their leaves, wildflowers with various pops of colour including reds, yellows, purples and blues. With every step you take, you notice something new, a bird busy in the trees and shrubs, a mouse or a shrew dart into the undergrowth of ivy or brambles – everywhere you turn, there Is life.

As you continue to walk along the woodland path, you begin to hear the sound of water alongside the path. The gentle trickle of water, a stream running gently over stones and cobbles, which runs alongside you. You stop for a moment and watch the crystal-clear water, as the sun reflects off the surface. Take a deep breath in and as you breathe out, just notice how still you are, how calm and clear your mind is, just like the crystal-clear water in the stream.

Your gaze returns to the woodland path, and you can see up ahead there are three steps in the bank which lead you down to water. You begin to walk towards the steps and on reaching the steps, you take a deep breath in and as you breathe out, you step down the steps, sitting on the bottom step.

You sit and rest for a while. You take off your shoes and socks and let your toes and feet dip into the cool water, noticing how good it feels as the cool, smooth water rushes over your skin. You can smell the fresh water intermingled with the smell of the plants and the wildflowers in the woodland that surround you.

As you sit there, at the edge of the stream, with your feet dipped into the cooling water, surrounded by nature, you look to the other side of the stream, across to the bank opposite you and there appears an animal. If you do not see an animal, that is absolutely fine. It means that in this moment, you are completely at peace and exactly where you need to be.

If you do see an animal on the opposite side of the stream, the animal remains completely still and makes eye contact with you. As you look into the animal's eyes and it looks back into yours, you may feel a connection, you may experience feelings or emotions pass between you and the animal. You may have flashes of images, hear a word or you may experience complete peace and stillness. Perhaps you feel nothing at all, and that's okay.

Just spend the next few moments maintaining eye contact with the animal and noticing that as you breathe in, the animal breathes in and the same when you breathe out. The animal is in complete unison with you, you are connected fully with nature in this moment – enjoy it.

After a few minutes, you take a deep breath in and as you exhale, the animal breaks its gaze and moves off into the woodland. In this moment, as you watch the animal return to the woodland, you may experience a sense of loss or longing for it to return, or perhaps you feel privileged that you have had this unique moment and connection with the animal.

Whatever you feel right now, just know that you have just encountered your spirit animal and that it has always been alongside you, guided you, supporting you. And know that your spirit animal will always appear to you whenever you need guidance, reassurance or just a complete connection with nature.

You take a last look at the clear stream, as the sun reflects off the surface of the water, which trickles gently over the pebbles at the bottom of the stream. You take a deep breath in, and ask you breathe out, you stand up and begin to walk up the three steps in the side of the bank and your feet are instantly dry and your socks and shoes back on.

You begin to walk back along the woodland path, making your way back to where you started. You pass the wildflowers, trees, ferns and mosses, noticing birds and small mammals still busy in the woodland.

Step by step and breath by breath, you make your way all the way back to where you started until you are back in the middle of the woodland, surrounded by trees, surrounded by nature.

And knowing you can always return, whenever you need to, to find the stream and dip your feet in the cooling water, to connect with your spirit animal, then when you are ready, you can take five deep breaths and open your eyes.

The Log Cabin
(Easily adapted for daytime or evening).

A Wild Minds' original: for when you need to feel cared for, valued, loved and held. A meditation to make you feel warm and understood.

We begin as we always do, training our mind and body to work as one and to slow down by taking our five deep breaths, in through the nose and out through the mouth.

If you can in your mind, you imagine yourself in a woodland, a woodland of your choice. Perhaps the woodland is familiar to you, perhaps it is completely from your imagination. Whatever you see is absolutely fine.

It is early evening in your woodland, with the sun beginning to set around you. The woodland is still and peaceful with trees of every shape and colour. You see the white bark of the Sliver Birch, the deep plum bark of Cherry trees and the rough grooved bark and twisted branches of gnarly, old Oak trees. Even if you do not know the names of the trees around you, you can tell they are all different by the shape of their leaves, the colour and texture of their bark and how they have grown.

You can see animals in your woodland too, perhaps rabbits and squirrels, bird life all around, maybe in foxes and deer brave enough to show themselves to you as they know you pose no threat and are welcome in their woodland.

As you stand there in the woodland, still and peaceful and content, you take a deep breath in and as you breath in, you can smell wood smoke, sweet and inviting, drifting through the woodland and as you breathe out, you feel your whole body relax and let go.

The sweet scent of wood smoke calls you and pulls you towards the direction in which it comes from. You take another deep breath in, and as your breath out, you allow yourself to begin to walk through the woodland, with the scent of wood smoke as you guide, knowing you will find wherever it is you need to be by following the sweet, comforting scent.

You continue to walk through the woodland, not following a set path, but allowing yourself to be guided through dense woodland and on each inbreath smelling that scent of wood smoke. You may pass streams and small waterfalls, rocks, ferns and mosses, wildflowers and animals. You feel the ground come up to meet your feet with each step, sure and solid. You feel safe, you feel held and supported by the woodland and you know the wood smoke will guide you.

As you continue to walk, the scent of wood smoke grows stronger, and you can see up ahead a clearing in the woodland. As you continue and reach the clearing, you find yourself in a beautiful glade, a clearing in the woodland where grass grows and the evening can reach the ground fully, bringing light and warmth. In the clearing, there is also a log cabin.

You can see that the wonderful, sweet, wood smoke you can smell is coming from the chimney of the log cabin. The log cabin has a small veranda on the front of it and on the veranda is a rocking chair covered with a blanket.

You can see from where you stand that there is a warm glow from inside the log cabin and you that it is warm and cosy in there. You take a deep breath in, and on your outbreath, you begin to walk towards the log cabin, making your way up the steps to the veranda and reaching the log cabin door. As you stand there, feeling the warmth that radiates from the log cabin, you reach into your pocket and find a key in there. You remove the key from your pocket and notice the beautiful patterns and shapes on the old key. You know instinctively that this key will unlock the log cabin door for you.

Taking another deep breath in, as you exhale you place the key in the log on the door of the cabin, unlock the door, open it and step inside the log cabin, closing the door softly behind you.

Inside the log cabin is a beautiful log fire, and you can smell the sweet wood smoke that you have followed all the way through the woodland. The log cabin is warm and safe and is full of things you love. Perhaps there are books to read, films to watch, blankets and pillows to make you comfortable. Perhaps there is your favourite meal cooking on the old stove, your favourite drink ready and waiting for you on the wooden table. Everything you love and enjoy you can find within your log cabin.

You spend the next few minutes enjoying your log cabin, feeling the sensation of love and warmth. You deserve to feel loved and cared for and right now in this moment, the woodland and log cabin which has called you to it are wrapping themselves around you like a big hug. You are wonderful and unique and the woodland and log cabin share with you just how special you are and how much they care for you and guide you.

After you have had some time enjoying the log cabin, it is time to leave. Leaving can be difficult, as who would want to leave a place where they feel so cared for and loved. But know that the log cabin is yours and your alone and that you can return whenever you need to. Whenever you need to feel safe, loved and celebrated, whenever you need a hug.

The log cabin with its sweet wood smoke is always there for you and only you have the key. When you are ready, you take a deep breath in and make your wait out of the log cabin, closing the door gently behind you and locking it with the beautiful old key from your pocket.

You have this key with you always and you can return to the cabin whenever you need to. The wood burner in the log cabin remains on and is of no threat to the cabin, remaining safely burning to keep everything cosy for you.

You begin to make your way down the steps and off the veranda and begin to walk away from the clearing, taking a last look at the log cabin, with the smell of sweet wood smoke still all around. You take a deep breath in and as you breathe out, you begin to make your way back towards the woodland, knowing you can easily find your way all the way back to where you started your journey. Passing streams and small waterfalls, rocks and ferns and mosses, wildflowers and wildlife.

Eventually, you make your way all the way back to where you started, surrounded by trees as the evening sun sets slowly around you, with birds, rabbits, squirrels and deer.

With a sense of love and contentment throughout your whole body, you take five deep breaths and slowly open your eyes, coming back to the present.

South American Meditations

Our South American meditations and themed "deep dive" sessions have proved very popular over the last year. We would like to share with you some of our favourite and most vividly experienced meditations and hope that you like them as much as we like delivering them. Although these meditations are based on Andean traditions and belief systems, learnt through our time in the Peruvian Amazon with native people, these meditations are all the creation of Wild Minds and have offered a deep meditative experience for us which is why we enjoy delivering them to others.

Our South American mediations enable you to fully connect with Pachamama (Mother Earth) and have the potential to connect with previous lives, sometimes going back for centuries. It is not unusual to see vivid colours or experience a sense of movement during these mediations as they are able to take you to a deeper state, allowing your brain to work using Theta or Delta waves, which are the gate way between conscious and unconscious.

It is whilst in this deep state, that participants of our group session often experience collective components, for example all visualising the full meditation in black and white, or perhaps having the same person or animal revealed to them. This collective meditative state is a rare and amazingly connective experience. Science suggests this state occurs when people have meditated together for a while and when the heart and breath rate of individuals synchronises complete connectedness in nature.

If you wish to experience the full multi-sensory experience this mediation's can offer, then join one of our Wild Minds South American sessions.

The Mud Hut

Begin with our five deep breath technique to start, following the journey of air as it enters your nose, moves down into your throat and lungs, inflating your belly and expanding your ribcage. Following the reverse journey as you breathe out and the air leaves your lungs, your ribcage and all the muscles relax, your belly flattens, and the warm breath leaves your mouth.

Once you reach your fifth breath, just take five more in exactly the same way, knowing with each long outbreath you are lowering your heart rate, lowering your blood pressure and helping everything to slow down.

Imagine yourself, if you can, in a woodland, bathed in sunlight. Trees surround you and you can feel a sense of peace and tranquility as you take in all the sights, sounds and sensations that nature has to offer you.

You hear birds in the trees and see a variety of other woodland animals which inhabit your woodland, all busy going about their everyday life, happy and safe in the knowledge that you are there. You take a deep breath in, and as you breathe out you notice a path that has appeared in your woodland. This path is yours to take, in order to begin your journey to connecting fully with who you truly are.

You take another deep breath in, and as you exhale, you begin to walk along the woodland path, feeling the ground coming up to meet your feet with each step. You feel stillness, you feel hope and you feel a sense of adventure within you.

As you continue to walk along the woodland path, you begin to notice, as your eyes adjust to the beautiful shards of orange and yellow sunlight breaking through the tree canopy above, that your woodland is changing. The trees around you are more tropical and jungle-like, with large exotic fronds and unusual shapes and patterns to the leaves and bark. The birds that you can hear and see are brightly coloured and vibrant, more like macaws and hummingbirds.

The woodland is becoming more jungle-like and ancient with each step you take, becoming ever denser with wild shrubs and unusual trees, as well as exotic animals which you have never before encountered. With each step, you can feel the history of the land on which you walk, and you feel each step is taking you further and further back in time, to meet your ancestors.

You can see up ahead in your jungle, that there is an archway in the trees where the jungle appears to stop, and you can see sunlight pouring through to the jungle floor. As you reach the edge of the jungle and exit through the archway, you find yourself on the edge of a riverbank. The riverbank is a sandy red colour, and the water runs gently and steadily in front of you.

You can smell the damp, humid smell of your ancient jungle and yet you can feel the cool breeze from the river as it flows gently passed. On the edge of the river, resting up against the bank, you see an old wooden canoe. You know in that moment that you are about to embark on an adventure which will connect you both with history and nature, a journey to open your mind and heart even further than it already is.

You make your way towards the old canoe and when you reach it you can see that there are no oars or paddles in the canoe and that you must trust in the river to get to your destination.

You inhale deeply and as you exhale, you step into the canoe, knowing you are safe, that the canoe will stay still and sturdy as you enter and that you will be guided by the river, sent by Pachamama (Mother Earth) to keep you safe and deliver you to your ancestors.

As you sit in the canoe, you take another deep breath in and as you breathe out, the canoe begins to move slowly but surely down the river. You can feel a cooling breeze on your face. Along the banks of the river, you can see the jungle, thick and dense, and you spot exotic animals resting by the banks of the river. Perhaps Puma and Cayman, Macaws and the great Harpy Eagle.

On the opposite side of the bank as you look at the red, sandy ground, you may see people. They appear pleased to see you and perhaps wave or smile. You feel instantly that you know these people. Perhaps they do not look like people you know, but they feel familiar and there is a connection between you, perhaps an ancient one. If you do not see people on the bank, that is absolutely fine, it means right now, in this moment, you are content, at ease and still.

Your canoe continues down the river and you can see up ahead there are three steps carved in to the red, sandy bank, which lead up on to the top bank. The canoe begins to move in the direction of this part of the bank and pulls up safely and securely on the bank by the three carved steps.

You take a deep breath in and as you breathe out, you step safely out of the old, wooden, canoe and you make your way up the three steps, which are carved into the red, sandy bank.

When you reach the top of the bank you can see an old mud hut in front of you. It is circular and made with straw and mud. It looks ancient and looks like it belongs here. You make your way to the mud hut towards a doorway which is covered by a thick animal-like hide. You place your hand on the mud hut and can feel the texture and temperature of it and know that you are about to experience something wonderful.

Taking another deep breath, as you exhale, you draw back the animal hide which covers the doorway and step inside. Inside the hut is beautiful, there are seats which have been intricately carved into a wooden bench which runs all the way along the inside of the mud hut. And in the middle of the room sits an old figure with an empty chair opposite them. The figure looks towards you and smiles, welcoming you into the mud hut and to their sacred place.

You sit opposite the old figure and although their face is etched with many lines, which tell stories of old, their eyes are bright and kind. They reach out to you with their open hands, and you place your hands in theirs, maintaining eye contact.

The moment your hands touch, you may see flashes of images, pictures, perhaps colours, sensations, feelings, a tingling throughout your body, perhaps words and song. Perhaps you feel, hear or see nothing at all, and that's ok.

Whatever you experience, you know that in this moment, you have found exactly where you need to be.

Just spend the next few moments enjoying the connection you have with the old figure sitting in front of you. Allow your mind, body and soul to connect with your ancestors, with Pachamama.

When you are ready, it is time to leave the mud hut and as always, leaving anywhere we feel completely at home, safe and loved can be difficult, but know that this community will always be here for you, as they have been here for you for your whole life and even before the life you live today. You will never feel alone again, knowing that you and only you can access this wonderful place where past meets present, surrounded by love and hope and acceptance.

You let go of the old figure's hands and they smile at you and nod, letting you know they understand you have to return to your present life, but that they know you will return.

Take a deep breath and as you exhale, you walk towards the hide that covers the doorway, move it to one side and step out of the mud hut and begin to make you wat towards the three steps which lead down to the river.

You know when you reach the riverbank, the old canoe will be there waiting for you. Just like before, when you reach the canoe, you step in, and it remains still and steady for you. Again, you need no oars or paddles, the canoe will gently lead you back upriver towards the archway in the trees which lead you back into the jungle.

Take your time making this journey, waving at the people on the bank once more if they appear and enjoying the wildlife you see enroute.

On reaching the other side of the riverbank, you step out of the canoe and make your way to the archway in the trees of the jungle. You take a last look at the river and the red, sandy riverbank before beginning to make your journey back through the dense, lush jungle, with its vibrant colours from flowers such as Bromeliads and the giant, deep green fronds of exotic plants and shrubs. Again, you pass trees, animals, birds you have never encountered before and you can smell the damp, humid jungle all around you.

As you continue to follow the path, you find yourself noticing that the jungle is becoming more woodland like with each step. Trees such as Silver Birch and Cherry return and the wildflowers are more familiar to you. The Macaws and Hummingbirds have gone and are replaced with Robins, Starlings and Blackbirds. The sun still shines through the trees and the birds still sing, but now they exist in a British woodland.

You continue to walk until you are right back where you started, in the woods, surrounded by trees, with life all around you and the sun gently breaking through the tree canopy above. Except now you carry a sense of everlasting love and care within you, you carry your ancestors with you always. And as you stand there, still and calm and complete, you look down to the palms of your hands and you may see perhaps a mark, a symbol or picture, a word or letter and this has been gifted to you by your ancestors, when the old figure held your hands. A reminder that you are loved that you belong and that you will always walk with their support and guidance within you.

And now, when you are ready, just take five deep breaths and open your eyes.

The Snake, the Puma and the Condor.

This meditation can be set in either morning, middle of the day or early evening and aims to connect you fully with Pachamama (Mother Earth) and enable you to feel content with what has past, what is present and what is yet to come. In order to do this, you will meet three very important animals in Andean culture: The Snake, The Puma and The Condor. The importance of these animals' dates back to the time of the Incas and can be seen in much of the Incan artwork and architecture and remains symbolic today across Peru.

Open your heart and mind and allow nature to guide you.

As always, begin with two repetitions of your five deep breaths, in through the nose and out through the mouth, placing yourself in a state in which your blood pressure and heart rate have lowered and where your mind and body begin to slow down. Knowing that every slow, deep breath will bring you closer to a deeper level of consciousness and a deeper understanding of yourself and your connection with nature.

You imagine yourself in a dense woodland, with trees of many differing shapes and sizes all around you. Trees with different colour bark and a range of patterns on their trunks, as well as varying shapes and sizes of the leaves which attach to each unique branch. The sunlight through the trees dances around on the woodland floor in front you off as it succeeds in breaking through the lush, dense canopy of leaves which tower high above you.

Although there is stillness and peace within your woodland, today you also feel an energy, a sense of electricity and magic waiting to happen. You know you are about to embark on an epic adventure, a journey which will connect all aspects of your being with Pachamama (Mother Earth).

As you stand there, in the woodland, you can hear the sound of birds in the trees around you and the rustle of small mammals in the ground-covering plants at the base of the trees. You feel peace, you feel hope and you feel alive.

Take a deep breath in and as you breathe out, you see a path appear before you, which slopes upwards slightly and leads you to higher ground within your woodland. The path is easy to walk, nothing strenuous or difficult. You climb further and further upwards as you continue along the woodland path.

You pass a range of beautiful wildflowers, shrubs, trees, ferns and mosses. Perhaps you notice streams and small waterfalls which filter through a range of rock structures around you. You notice a gentle breeze move through the woodland and the breeze encourages you to continue further along the path, to continue your journey and to experience full connection with Pachamama.

As you continue to walk along the woodland path, you notice that your woodland is changing. The trees around you are more tropical and jungle-like, with large exotic fronds and unusual shapes and patterns to the leaves and bark. The birds that you can hear and see are brightly coloured and vibrant, more like Macaws and Hummingbirds.

The woodland is becoming more jungle-like and ancient with each step you take, becoming ever denser with wild shrubs and unusual trees, as well as exotic animals which you have never before encountered. With each step, you can feel the history of the land on which you walk. You spot brightly coloured flowers such as Bromeliads with bright pink, orange and yellow flowers, perhaps Orchids and Flytraps. The environment is more humid, and you can feel the warmth and moisture on your skin.

Eventually, your path levels off and you can see up ahead that the jungle ends with an archway in the trees, and at the end of the jungle, you reach a plateau, a rocky outcrop on which there stands a large stone altar. The altar is made of two large boulders and a large slab of flat rock across the top of the two boulders. As you exit the jungle and step onto the rocky plateau and stand in front of the stone altar, you can see the most spectacular view. A view of mountains as far as the eye can see, a vast expanse of towering mountains, with many of them covered in trees. These trees make up a very unique habitat called a Cloud Forest, and they are dense, lush, humid and full of adventure, just like your jungle.

The view is stunningly beautiful, and you take a deep breath in, capturing everything you see, hear, smell and feel past, present and future at the stone altar, knowing you are special to have been guided to this phenomenally sacred and rare place. You know whatever you encounter in this wonderful place will help to enlighten you, to guide you and to immerse you in nature fully.

You take another deep breath in and as you breathe out you look toward the stone altar in front of you and there appears a snake. The snake is not there to harm you or frighten you. It remains calm and barely moving but makes eye contact with you. The snake is there to connect you with the underworld, the ground beneath you. The underworld is not linked with death or grief but with the past. The snake represents all of the things that make you who you are today.

The experiences, conversations, loves and losses that have shaped who you are and have led you to be the person you are today. You take another deep breath in and as you breathe out, you reach out to touch the snake, knowing the snake will never hurt you.

As your fingers make contact with the skin of the snake, you may experience flashes of images, people, places; you may feel emotions, a connection. The snake is there to remind you of all the wonderful things that have shaped you and to remind you that despite the negative things you may have encountered in your life, that you are strong, constant and alive. The snake is there to tell you how proud you should be of who you are and where you have come from. The snake is sent as a reminder to be kind to yourself, and to let who you are shine.

You take a deep breath in and as you breathe out, the snake has gone. Your gaze returns to the beautiful mountain range before you, covered in cloud forests, with the sounds of the jungle all around you. You are safe, you are still, and you are strong.

Take another deep breath in and as you breathe out, a Puma appears before you, standing on its hind legs with its front paws on the altar in front of you. Again, the Puma is of no threat to you and has the most beautiful eyes you have ever seen. Take another breath and as you breathe out, reach out and place your hand on of the Puma's paws.

Again, as you make contact with the Puma, you may experience flashes of images, people, places, feel a range of emotions. Know that you are safe, and that the puma is there to help you to celebrate who you are right now in this moment. The Puma is sent to remind you to stay present with the world around you, to be proud of what you achieve every day and to find joy and contentment in the here and now.

The Puma reminds you just how wonderful you are and provides you with an overwhelming sense of love and acceptance. Regardless of the hand you have been dealt and the challenges you may have encountered, you are still standing strong today, breathing in and out, steady and constant, you are amazing. Enjoy the next few moments as you connect with the Puma and the present and a celebration of you and your achievements, the feeling of life.

You take a deep breath in and as you breath out, the Puma has gone. Your gaze returns to the beautiful mountain range before you, covered in cloud forests, with the sounds of the jungle all around you. You are safe, you are still, and you are strong, and you carry a sense of love and belonging within you and all around you.

Take another deep breath in and as you breathe out, your attention is drawn to a large Condor, a beautiful bird of prey, circling in the sky above the mountains and cloud forest you see before you. The Condor is free, full of energy and hope as it circles high above you. You notice that the Condor has made eye contact with you, and it turns towards you in the air and brings itself to a graceful landing on the stone altar in front of you.

The Condor gazes into your eyes as it sits on the altar, occasionally tilting its head to the side as it does. As you take a further deep breath in, and breathe out, you reach out to touch the feathers on the wings of the Condor and feel an energy, a feeling of excitement and hope, possibilities, and dreams. Again, you may experience a warmth or a tingling, a buzz of energy pass between you and the Condor.

The Condor represents your future and everything you are destined to become. The hopes and ambitions you may have, everything you wish to feel and achieve is possible when you take time to remember just how incredible you are, how when you put your mind to anything, you can achieve it.

You take another deep breath in and as you breathe out, the Condor turns away from you and spreads its wings out, displaying the giant wingspan of these truly beautiful bird of prey. You take a further deep breath in and as you breath out you stretch your arms out to the side, as if you have the wings of the Condor. You find yourself taking a further breath in and on your outbreath, you push off from the stone altar and you fly high and soar into the sky above the mountains and cloud forests, as you are now the Condor.

You feel light and yet powerful, free and determined, full of hope, love and strength. Spend the next few minutes enjoying the fight of the Condor across the ancient landscape, knowing anything is possible if you believe in yourself and all you are destined to be, allowing nature to guide you every step of the way.

Now, it is time to return to the stone altar and so you, the Condor, turn towards the mountainside where you stood by the altar, surrounded by forest and mountain. Bring yourself into a gentle and graceful land on to the stone altar and you find yourself instantly back, as you once more as you stand there and watch the Condor take flight once more, circling high above you, willing you on to succeed and to be true to who you are.

You take a last look at the stunning view in front of you, knowing that you can always return whenever you need to, to connect with your past, your present and your future and to remind yourself just how unique and wonderful you truly are. You make your way back into the jungle, through the archway in the trees and begin to make your way, this time downhill, back along the path through the humid jungle.

Back past the plants and trees with their large exotic fronds and unusual shapes and patterns to the leaves and bark. Past the brightly coloured birds such as macaws and hummingbirds.

Past the brightly coloured flowers such as Bromeliads with bright pink, orange and yellow flowers, perhaps orchids and flytraps.

As you continue to walk back down the path, gently and surely, you notice the jungle has become more woodland-like and the trees and animals which inhabit it, more familiar to a British woodland. With Oak, Silver Birch and Cherry trees, with Robins and Blackbirds and wildflowers such as Oxeye Daisies and Forget-Me-Nots.

Until you find yourself all the way back where you started, in a dense woodland, with trees of many differing shapes and sizes all around you. The sunlight through the trees dances around on the woodland floor in front you off as it succeeds in breaking through the lush, dense canopy of leaves which tower high above you, just as it did at the start.

As well as stillness and peace within you and the woodland, you now carry within you a sense of strength, shared with you when you connected with the snake, the link to the underground, a reminder of everything that has shaped you and made you who you are today.

You also feel a sense of complete love and acceptance, shared with you and the Puma, a reminder of how strong and constant you are to be stood here today, breathing and full of life. feel an energy, a sense of electricity and magic waiting to happen.

And finally, a sense of hope and endless opportunities and possibilities, shared between you and the Condor, a reminder of just how brilliant you can and will be when you take time to celebrate and be kind to you, because you are unique, you are wonderful and nature, Pachamama accepts and loves you exactly as you are, and so should you.

And when you're ready, know your connection with Pachamama, Mother Earth, is stronger than ever and unbreakable, then when you're ready, take five deep breaths and open your eyes – take your time, there's no rush.

Message in box

Start as always with our five deep breaths, of which you are all now experts!

As you continue to breathe in that way, you find yourself in complete darkness apart from the stone staircase in front of you which leads downwards, with five steps.

You take a deep breath in and as you breathe out, you step down and count "five".
On the next deep breath in, as you breathe out, again you step down and count "four".
You breathe in and breathe out, step down and count "three".
Again, breathe in slowly and deeply and as you breathe out, step down and count "two".
Breathe in, breathe out and step down, counting "one".

As you breathe in again and breathe out, stepping down the final step and counting one, you find yourself faced with a beautifully carved wooden door, with patterns, shapes, symbols, faces, and animals carved into it. You run your fingers in the grooves of the patterns and trace the designs across the door with your finger.

You take another deep breath in and prepare to explore what is behind the amazingly beautiful door, and on breathing out, you open the door, step through it and close the door behind you.

You find yourself in the lushest, most densely rich forest you have ever experienced. Everything is so vibrant in colour, plants and trees of various shapes, sizes and colours. Some species you have never seen before, and they appear unusual and exotic, full of vibrance and life.

As well as the brightly coloured trees, shrubs and flowers all around, there are birds and animals bright in colour and you can feel their energy all around you.

You can hear the breeze blowing gently in the trees around you and sunlight dances on the forest floor where the sun breaks through the lush green leaves all around you on the trees.

There appears to be no obvious path in this beautiful, deep, and ancient forest, but you know exactly where to go. You take a deep breath and centre your focus on a pull you feel from the centre of your chest, from your heart and as you breathe out you find yourself walking in the direction you are drawn to. You know that there is location deep within this beautiful landscape, which calls to you and urges you to walk toward it. The breeze encourages you to continue and guides you steadily and surely to where you need to be.

You enjoy every step you take within this deep forest, and you find excitement and new experiences at every turn: the sweet smell of new flowers, the earthy smell of giant mushrooms, ferns and mosses which cover large areas of tree trunks and the ground around you.

Eventually, you find yourself pulled towards a particular tree within this stunning forest. Perhaps the largest tree or the most unusual in the forest, whatever type of tree it is you see, this tree calls to you and pulls you towards it, like an imaginary cord from your heart to the tree.

As you approach the tree, you stop and breathe deeply several times and you can feel the tree breathing with you. On each inhale you take; you can feel the tree breathe in deeply with you and the same on each out breathe. You are connected in so many ways to this wonderful, majestic tree.

You feel drawn towards this tree and know that as soon as you place your hands on its bark, that you will experience a rush of emotion, strength, love and belonging. Like a long-lost friend or loved one, you know this tree by heart, and it knows you. Just spend the next few moments as you connect with the tree, noticing how the bark feels under the palm of your hands, hugging the tree if you wish you, placing your face onto the bark and feeling the tree breathe with you.

When you are ready, you take a step back from the tree and trace your eyes all the way from the roots which enter the ground, up the trunk of the tree, noticing it barks, any patterns and shapes, scars and new growth. Continue to trace your eyes upwards to the branches, twigs and leaves until you see the very top of the tree canopy of your tree.

And now, allow you gaze to move slowly back down your tree until they make their way back towards the bottom of the trunk, where you now notice a small door in the base of the trunk. You kneel and gently open the small door in the base of the trunk.

Behind the door is a small space, in which sits an old wooden box. You take a deep breath in and as you breathe out, you reach in and retrieve the little wooden box. Just like the door that brought you to this magical forest, the old wooden box is too beautifully carved with designs, shapes, symbols, words, faces and perhaps animals. Just like with the door, you trace your fingers over the patterns and designs, enjoying the beauty of the box.

Take another deep breath in and the breathing out, you open the little, old, wooden box and find inside a message. Perhaps a piece of paper or a stone with a word, a written message, a symbol, a shape or perhaps a face or animals drawn on it. Perhaps the box is empty and instead you receive an emotion, a feeling or perhaps you hear a message on the breeze as you open the box. Perhaps you see, feel or hear nothing at all and that's ok. That means you are simply content with the stillness in your heart and mind that you currently are experiencing.

If you do receive a message in the form of paper or stone or a written in some way, you are free to place this message in your pocket or to return it to the box, knowing you carry the message in your heart and that it will always remain with you.

After a few moments, you take a deep breath in and close the lid of the old, wooden box and as you breath out, you return the old box to the space within the tree and close the lisle wooden door in the base of the trunk.

You stand back up and enjoy looking at your tree once more, the tree which called you to it from afar, the tree that has seen many changes through history but has remained strong and constant, the tree that knows you inside out and loves and welcomes you no matter what.

This tree knows your deepest secrets, your deepest pains and your greatest achievements and this tree will remain with you always as your connection with nature.

It is now time to leave you tree, and leaving a friend or loved is always hard, but know that you will be able to find your tree whenever you need to feel accepted, understood and loved, whenever you need to feel at home and at peace and whenever you might need guidance and direction.

You take a deep breath once more and as you breathe out, you walk back through the forest, making your way back to where you started. Passing birds and trees, plants and animals which are perhaps new to you, vibrant in colour, sound and scent. You belong in this wonderful forest, and you are always welcome here, anytime you need guidance, peace and hope.

Step by step and breath by breath, you find yourself back in front of the wooden door, intricately carved with designs and once more, you trace the designs with your finger.

And it is now time to leave this magical forest, knowing the door remains unlocked for you and only you, always. You take another deep breath and as you breathe out, you open the carved door, step through, finding yourself at the bottom of the stone staircase, and close the door behind you.

This time, carrying the message or stillness you received within your heart, you take a deep breath in and as you breathe out, you step up the first step and count "one".

Take another breath in, breathe out, step up the next step and count "two".

Continue to breathe in this way, breathing in deeply and on each out breath stepping up, three and then four and five until you are back at the top of the staircase, and on reaching the top, you can open your eyes.

Meditations for Fun

Meditation does not have to take hours or require you to sit still for long periods of time in serious contemplation. At Wild Minds, we understand and celebrate that everyone is unique and what works for one person may not work for another. Therefore, we always try to offer a mixture of the traditional and quirky!

The following meditations are creations of Wild Minds and are certainly entertaining, a little bit out there and wonderful for those of us who like to allow our minds time to be creative and to find that inner child again.

Perfect for those with shorter attention spans and guaranteed to leave a smile on your face.

Parachuting Ants

Close your eyes and you find yourself in the centre of a woodland, surrounded by trees of all different shapes, sizes and colours.

In front of you there is a large fallen log on which you can see deep grooves in the bark and moss and ivy growing on parts of the log. As you look at the log, from left to right, you take a closer look and notice that there is an army of ants marching along the log, walking in one of the grooves in the bark.

As each ant reaches the end of the log, it jumps down and makes its way vertically up the trunk of the nearest tree, right at the end of the fallen log. Each ant continues up the side of the standing tree until it reaches a junction on the tree, where some ants turn left and make their way across a branch of the tree, and some of the ants continue upwards until they are out of view, above the tree canopy.

You continue to watch the ants who turned along the branch and you watch them carefully. As they reach the end of the branch, where the smaller trigs hold delicate leaves, each ant pulls off a single leave and jumps off the end of the twig on which it stands, using the leaf above its head as a parachute.

Each ant then makes a slow and fun descent to the woodland floor, where they drop their leaves and head back to the start of the fallen log for another go. You watch ant after ant continue to enjoy this fun and exciting activity in the woodland, with smiles on their faces, laughing and joking as they march.

You take a deep breath in and as you breathe out, you find yourself as an ant, now included in the line of marching ants, making your way along the fallen log, walking inside one the groove in the bark, following the cheery ant in front of you.

As you reach the end of the log, you jump down and then make your way vertically up the tree trunk in front of you, just like the ant friend in front of you. With a smile on your face, you continue up the trunk with ease and with a bound in your step.

You now find yourself at the choice of either turning left along the branch or you can continue to a higher branch, by continuing up the tree trunk, above the tree canopy and taking the jump from a higher point.

Whichever you choose, you find yourself now marching along a branch, leading to twigs holding delicate leaves. You watch the ant in front of you pick a leave, hold it above their head and jump on the twig, making their way safely back to the ground.

And now it's your turn. You reach up to a leave above your head, pick it, hold it above your head like a canopy and you take a deep breath in and as you breathe out, you smile and jump off the twig.

You sway side to side gently, gliding easily and carefully all the way down, alongside the tree until you land with grace and ease on the woodland floor, with a smile and carrying joy and excitement within you.

You take three deep breaths in, knowing you will carry the sense of joy and excitement with you all day and on your third breath, you open your eyes.

Leaf Boats

You imagine yourself standing on the bank of a river in the bright, warm sunlight. The water in the river passes you by gently and steadily, and the sunlight reflects beautifully off the surface of the water.

You can see plants and reeds along the edge of the river both where you stand and across the river on the other side of the bank. You take a deep breath in and as you breathe out you see a small leaf boat come into view on the river. The leaf boat is a tiny boat made of leaves which can fit in the palm of your hand.

As the leaf boat comes into view and floats by in front of you, you can see there is a frog in the leaf boat, sitting on a little stool, reading a paper. You watch the frog in his leaf boat, sail on by and you take a deep breath in and as you breathe out you feel relaxed and happy.

As you stand there, in the warming sunlight, which reflects off the surface of the water in the river, you take another deep breath in and as you breathe out, a second little leaf boat comes in to view on the river and begins to float in front of you.

A little boat made of leaves, which could fit in the palm of your hand. As the leaf boat passes in front of you, you can see inside this leaf boat, is a little mouse, laying on his back with sunglasses on and his arms above his head.

You watch the little mouse float on by and feel joy and happiness as you breath in and out.

As you stand there, in the warming sunlight, which reflects off the surface of the water in the river, you take another deep breath in and as you breathe out, a third little leaf boat comes in to view on the river and begins to float in front of you.

As the little boat made of leaves passes in front of you, you can see two small bank voles with oars in their hands, paddling with speed and energy as they race down the river. You take a deep breath in and feel excitement and joy as you breathe out and the banks voles race on by.

As you stand there, in the warming sunlight, which reflects off the surface of the water in the river, you take another deep breath in and as you breathe out, a final little leaf boat comes in to view on the river and begins to float in front of you.

This leaf boat is for you. You take a deep breath in and as you breathe out you find yourself in the leaf boat and now it's your turn to decide how you want to move down the river in your little boat made of leaves.

You can sit on a stool like the little frog and read the newspaper or a book. You can be like the mouse on his back with his arms behind his head and his sunglasses on or you can race down the river with the little oars.

However, you choose to move down the river, you move with peace and joy and a smile on your face. You continue to move down river in that for a few moments and then the little leaf boat slowly comes to rest on the bank once more. You take a deep breath in and when you breathe out you are you again on the bank of the river, with the sun shining down, with a smile on your face and joy in your heart.

Take three deep breaths and you can open your eyes, carrying joy and energy with you all day.

Woodland Riviera

Take five deep breaths, in through the nose and out through the mouth and on your fifth breath, you find yourself in a woodland, surrounded by trees, surrounded by nature.

You are surrounded by trees of all different shapes and sizes, but there is one particular tree that grabs your attention. Something that calls to you from a particular tree, perhaps the colour or shape of the leaves, perhaps it's the tallest or twistiest tree in the woodland. Whatever it is, you find yourself walking towards this tree which calls you.

As you reach the tree, you notice that there is a door in the base of the trunk, a door large enough for you to pass through. You know that you have been called to this tree for a reason and that everything you need can be found through the door.

Take a deep breath in, and as you breathe out, you open the door in the trunk of the tree and you step inside the tree, closing the door behind you and you are instantly transported through the tree to a secluded, beautiful beach – your woodland riviera.

You are greeted by a frog with a towel draped over his arm and a menu in the other hand. The frog smiles at you and waves the arm with the towel to a chair with a table and parasol to shade you from the warming sun.

You take a seat at the table and take the menu off the frog, seeing that the menu holds your favourite food and drink. You select a drink and a snack and pass the menu back to the smiling frog.

As you sit there in your woodland riviera, you notice that the sea, on which the sun sparkles as it reflects, has a number of water-loving animals enjoying themselves within it. There are otters playing water polo and lazing on inflatables, there are frogs on yachts sailing across the beautiful, clear water, there are fish snorkeling and coming up for air. Everywhere you look there is laughter and fun in the sea.

You take a deep breath in and as you breathe out, your attention is drawn to the sandy shore where all animals who love to burrow and dig are enjoying the sand. Foxes and rabbits dig holes and build sandcastles together happily, badgers and moles tunnel along the beach to the sea, allowing water into forts they have built, all another around is laughter and fun on the beach.

You take another deep breath in and as you breathe out, your attention is caught by all the flying animals enjoying taking a running jump off a nearby branch of a tree, which overhangs the sea. Kingfishers and Herons, Bats and Butterflies, all take time to race towards the end of the branch and laugh into flight, swooping low across the surface of the glistening sea.

The woodland riviera is full of energy, life and laughter. Your attention is drawn back to the table in front of your which now has your favourite drink and snack upon it. You take a bite to eat and a sip of your drink. You take a deep breath in and as you breathe out, you stand up and make your way to the edge of the shore, where the sea meets the sand, and you feel the warm water lapping gently over your feet. As you take another deep breath, you hear every animal in the woodland riviera breathe in with you and as you turn around, you see every animal lined up on the beach behind you and as you breathe out, they breathe out with you.

Every animal breathes in time with you, and they wait patiently on the sand as you find your feet. You take another deep breath in and as you breathe out, you turn and dive into the water and the animals all around begin to play just as they were before, happy in the knowledge that you have joined them in the woodland riviera.

Spend as long as you need playing, relaxing and enjoying this unique and joyful place and when you are ready, take three deep breaths and open your eyes.

Lily pads

Begin as we always do, with five deep breaths, in through the nose and out through the mouth, allowing your heart rate to slow and your blood pressure to drop. Allowing everything to slow down a little.

Imagine yourself, if you can, standing on the edge of a large pond. The sun is shining down and reflects of the surface of the water and from where you stand on the edge of the pond, you can see that there are a series of large Lily pads which start near you side of the pond and continue all the way across the surface of the pond, reaching the opposite side of the pond to yourself.

You take a deep breath in, and as you breathe out, you look to your side and there, has appeared a frog. The frog looks you in the eye and look into his and the frog smiles and nods his head at you and you know what the frog must do.

The frog jumps onto the first lily pad, the lily pad dips gently below the surface of the water but bounces back up as it supports the weight of the frog and the frog continues to leap from lily pad to lily pad to lily pad until he has made it all the way to the other side of the pond, where he stops and turns to look at you.

The frog looks you in the eye and you look in his and you smile and nod at the frog and you know what you must do.

You take a deep breath in and as you breathe out, you jump onto the first lily pad and it dips below the surface of the water and bobs back up again, supporting your weight and you continue across the pond, jumping from lily pad to lily pad to lily pad, with joy in your heart and spring in your step, until you are all the way across the pond where to stop and turn around and look at the frog next to you.

As you stand there at the edge of the pond, with the sun shining down and warming you, you look at the frog and he looks at you and you both smile and nod your heads, and you know what you must do.

You take a deep breath in and when you breathe out, you and the fog take each other's hand and you jump together from lily pad to lily pad to lily pad with smiles on your faces and joy in your hearts, until you are all the way back to the original side of the pond, where you stop and face the pond, standing hand in hand with the frog in the sun.

You and the frog look at each other and smile and with joy in your heart and a smile on your face, you take three deep breaths and open your eyes.

Short Meditations

Floating on the Stream

Imagine you are sitting or standing in the middle of a stream.
The water is flowing away in front of you.
Notice if there is any sound from the running water.
Notice if there are any trees, etc. on the banks of the stream.

Now see leaves floating down the stream away from you.
They can be any shape, colour, or size.
As the negative thoughts come into your mind, be aware of what the thought is, and then place it on a leaf.

Now watch it float away down the stream.

Do this with each thought as you notice it and for as long as you like until you feel better.

As you acknowledge each of your thoughts, you do not need to hang onto them.

There is no need to become attached to the thought.

Just acknowledge it and then place it on a leaf.

By watching it float away, it loses its hold on you and its intensity.

The Flower

As you sit, in a comfortable position, take a moment to acknowledge your breath. Don't change anything about it, just become aware of it as it flows in and out of your body.

Now visualise a small flower bud sitting in the palm of your hand. It is tiny and all closed up on itself.

As you continue to breathe in and out the flower begins to grow. With each out breath a petal begins to unfurl.

Breathe in and out as you flower opens up in your palm. Petal by petal becoming a beautiful bloom in your hand.

Your flower is in full bloom. You acknowledge its beauty and the journey it has been on you get to this point and you reflect back that journey on yourself.

You too have been on a journey, growing one petal at a time to reach this point in your life. You are a beautiful bloom, a flower of significant individuality and purpose.

With your breath allow the flower to float up into the air in front of you. Let the bloom travel on in its journey as you will travel on in yours.

Meditations for Savasana

Savasana is one of the most important parts of your Yoga practice. It helps you control your parasympathetic nervous system, and this helps you feel calm, relaxed and allows your brain time to file and prepare for what is to come.

Our savasana scripts will help you on a journey that will encourage better mood regulation and enhance the benefits of the whole of Yoga.

Take Flight

Come to lie in Savasana (Corpse Pose), with your arms relaxed at the side of your body and your feet and legs relaxed on the ground.

Begin by releasing your breath and relaxing into the ground beneath you.

Become aware of your breath as you relax further and release all tension from your body. Your muscles are so relaxed that it feels like you are floating.

Bring into your mind's eye a beautiful blue lake, you are floating on this lake. The lake is surrounded by forests and mountains. The sky is blue above you; the sun shines down on to your body and fluffy white clouds drift overhead.

You can feel the warmth of the sun as it touches your body. It brings a feeling of security and comfort to you. Underneath you, the water is cool, and its ripples tickle your skin as you bob around on the surface.

As you float there safe and relaxed, a breeze blows over you. The breeze lifts you and carries you to the shoreline and a small beach. The sand on the beach is soft between your toes and you see that the forest comes right down to the beach.

At the edge of the tree line, you see a small path leading into the forest. You decide to follow it..........

As you enter the forest the temperature around you reduces to cool. You notice that the sounds around you change, and the earthy smell of woodland enters your nostrils.

You begin to follow the path as it weaves its way between the trees. It is soft and mossy underfoot and you notice that it is starting to climb upwards. As you walk you can hear the sounds of the birds in the trees, the insects buzzing as they move and the breeze ruffling the branches above you.

The path continues upward, it is an easy walk, and you feel calm as you pass amongst the trees continuing on your journey. You notice that trees are starting to thin around and that the ground underfoot is beginning to become slightly rockier. Eventually the trees disappear behind you, and you are on the side of the mountain. Ahead of you the path continues, and you carry on walking. Climbing the mountain. Around you, the view has changed, and you can see the trees getting smaller and the mountain terrain becoming more visible.

In the distance you can see the summit, the top of the mountain. You continue to climb, over rocks and boulders. It is not a difficult climb as you are strong and confident. You take one final step and there you are, at the top of the mountain. Below you, you can see the forest, the tops of the trees highlighted by the sunshine. Looking out all around you are the mountains. The ones in the distance are snow-capped and bright. You take a moment to feel on top of the world, capable of anything and completely alive.

While you are taking in the view, an eagle flies past you. You feel it is calling you to follow. Without hesitation, you jump into the air and suddenly you are flying. Soaring through the air, around the mountain tops and over the trees. The wind in your face is exhilarating and you take in the whole scene below with a smile on your face. You circle above the trees and down and down toward the lake where you started your journey. The eagle dives and you follow it. You tuck in your arms/wings and break through the surface of the water.

Under the water, you notice an otter playing and swimming in and out of the reeds and weeds in the lake floor. You follow its lead and begin to swim, darting amongst the weeds and swimming with freedom and joy. As the otter comes to the surface for air, so do you. And there you are, back floating on the surface of the lake. Surrounded by forest and mountains. The sun is shining down on you. The blue sky above you and fluffy white clouds drifting overhead.

You take a moment to remember the feelings of excitement, joy, achievement. You are capable of anything you put your mind to. You are strong. You are special.

Remember all of this as you go on with the rest of your day.
Now take five deep breaths and when you are ready open your eyes, slowly come to a seated position and never forget this journey.

Namaste

The Warmth of Prana

Bringing yourself to lie comfortably in Savasana (Corpse Pose), you release all tension from your body.

Without bringing too much awareness to it, ensure that you are breathing naturally and filling your body with the life-giving prana. Bring awareness to the tip of your nose and the feeling of the air entering and exiting your nostrils.

Slowly begin to breathe into your toes, feeling the warmth enter this part of your body. Let that warmth travel to your feet and then your ankles. Enjoying the sensation of comfort that it gives you.

Allow your breath to fill the lower part of your legs, your knees and your thighs. Continuing this filling of the body with Prana; let your breath fill your buttocks and lower back. Be aware of the sensation as your breath fills your middle and upper back.

Let the warmth of your breath enter your shoulders and flow down through the upper arms, elbows, wrists, palms and fingers.

Taking a breath which will bring heat to your heart, let your breath fill your neck.

Slowly let your breath travel up through your chin, into your mouth flowing out into your cheeks and back into your nose.

Allow your breath to move through your eyelids and into your forehead. Coming to the end of this warming Prana exercise, breathe deeply into the top of your head.

Now, as you lie in this relaxed and warm position. Take a moment to reflect on the strength and power of your life force. Your Prana has filled your entire body with a loving warmth. It has focused your mind and given strength to your body.

Remaining in this position for a few moments and taking a few more breaths, begin to wiggle your fingers and your toes.

When you are ready return to a seated position.
Namaste

Yoga Nidra

This Yoga Nidra script can be read through before it is practiced. An audio version of this script is available to download from our website.

You will practice Yoga Nidra in Savasana (Corpse Pose), lying on your back.

Please take a moment to make yourself as comfortable as possible. Feel free to use a cushion, blanket or anything else to ensure your comfort during this practice.

Before you begin, bring into your mind's eye your sankalpa, your "I am" statement. Repeat it quietly and internally to yourself three times.

As you settle into Savasana, bring your awareness to the spaces between your body and the earth beneath you. Invite your body to relax and to melt into the ground. As you begin to give yourself over to relaxation, notice the spaces between your body and the earth beneath you becoming smaller and smaller. Your body relaxed, lying completely connected to the ground.

Shortly you will begin a rotation of awareness. All you have to do is allow your awareness to follow as we guide you from point to point within your body.

Right toes, left toes.
Right sole of foot, left sole of foot.
Right top of foot, left top of foot.
Right ankle, left ankle.
Right shin, left shin.
Right knee, left knee.
Right thigh, left thigh.
Right buttock, left buttock.
Groin.
Right hip, left hip.
Lower back.
Right fingers, left fingers.
Right hand, left hand.
Right wrist, left wrist.
Right forearm, left forearm.
Right elbow, left elbow.

Right upper arm, left upper arm.
Right shoulder, left shoulder.
Middle back.
Upper back.
Neck.
Chin
Bottom lip.
Tongue.
Upper Lip.
Right Cheek.
Nose.
Left cheek.
Right eyelid, left eyelid.
Right eye, left eye.
Right eyebrow, left eyebrow.
Forehead.
Right ear, left ear.
Back of the head.
Crown of the head.
Whole of the front of your body.
Whole of the back of your body.

Now bring your awareness to your breath. Become aware of the temperature of the air as it enters and exits your nostrils. Visualise the breath as a bright golden light that fills your body as you continue to breathe. Visualise your breath as it flows from the toes up through the legs, the body and into the head. Feel the warmth of this light fill your entire body.

Now imagine that you are standing barefoot at the edge of a lush green meadow. The meadow is bordered by beautiful hedgerows and the sounds of nature can be heard within them.

Ahead of you a path appears in the grass. You take your first step forward and begin to follow the path as it winds across the meadow. As your journey begins, more and more nature starts to appear around you and a woodland begins to form.

Your surroundings become greener and fuller in detail and texture. The trees and shrubs fill your vision and the smells of the woodland enter your nose.

The path beneath your feet is soft and you feel an energy coming from the earth on which you tread.

You reach the end of the path and there stands a large tree. There is a hole in it just at chest height and in the hole, there is a light. You look into the light and there you see your Sankalpa. The tree reinforces your Sankalpa and fills you with a feeling of strength and confidence.

Repeat your Sankalpa three more times.

Allow yourself to pause for five minutes.

Your practice of Yoga Nidra is now complete.

Slowly begin to bring awareness back to your physical body lying on the ground. Gently move the fingers and the toes.

When you are ready, come to a seated position.

Namaste

Journal

Reflections on Meditation

Acknowledgements

We would like to take this opportunity to say thank you to a few people, whom without, we wouldn't be where we are and have achieved what we have.

To our parents; Karen & Dave and Caroline & Steve. Obviously without them we wouldn't be here. But equally they have been really supportive as we started and continued on our crazy journey.

To the team at Moira Furnace Museum & Country Park. They allowed us to use their site when we first started. Not knowing what would happen or whether it would work. We hope that we can continue our relationship with you for years to come.

To all our loyal customers. Those who are with us week after week or those who we only see every now and then. We appreciate you all.

To our followers online. We have grown a wonderful community through nature over the past four years and hope that with this book you can feel more a part of it, even if you're not with us in person.

To you, the purchaser of this book, welcome to the Wild Minds family, thank you.

#connectingyouwithnature
#communitythroughnature
@wildmindsnature

Printed in Great Britain
by Amazon

42106318R00069